Legends

from Ancient Worlds

KINGSCOURT / McGRAW-HILL

Legends from Ancient Worlds

Copyright © 2002 Rigby Heinemann

Rigby is part of Harcourt Education, a division of
Reed International Books Australia Pty Ltd ABN 70 001 002 357.

Compiled by Jan Pritchett
Edited by Celia Purdey
Designed by Jennifer Johnston
Illustrated by Tony Albers, cover, pp. 8–13, 24; Laura Peterson, pp. 15–23

Acknowledgments
for photographs: © Richard Cummins/CORBIS/Australian Picture
Library, p. 4–5, 15; Master of the Campana Cassoni, *Theseus and the
Minotaur*, The Bridgeman Art Gallery, p. 7.
for text: David Higham Associates for the story "The Giants Who
Couldn't Swim" from *Realms of Gold: Myths and Legends From Around the World*
by Ann Pilling. Text © Ann Pilling 1993.

KINGSCOURT/McGRAW-HILL

Shoppenhangers Road, Maidenhead
Berkshire, SL6 2QL
Telephone: 01628 502730

Fax: 01628 635895

www.kingscourt.co.uk
E-mail: enquiries@kingscourt.co.uk

Printed in Australia by Advance Press

10 9 8 7 6 5 4 3 2 1

ISBN: 0-07-710341-6

Contents

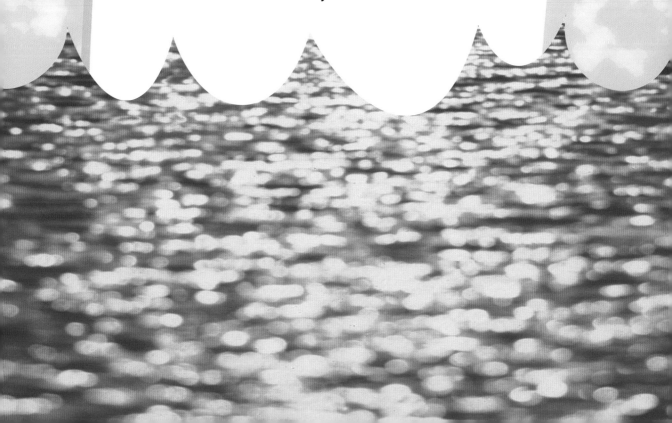

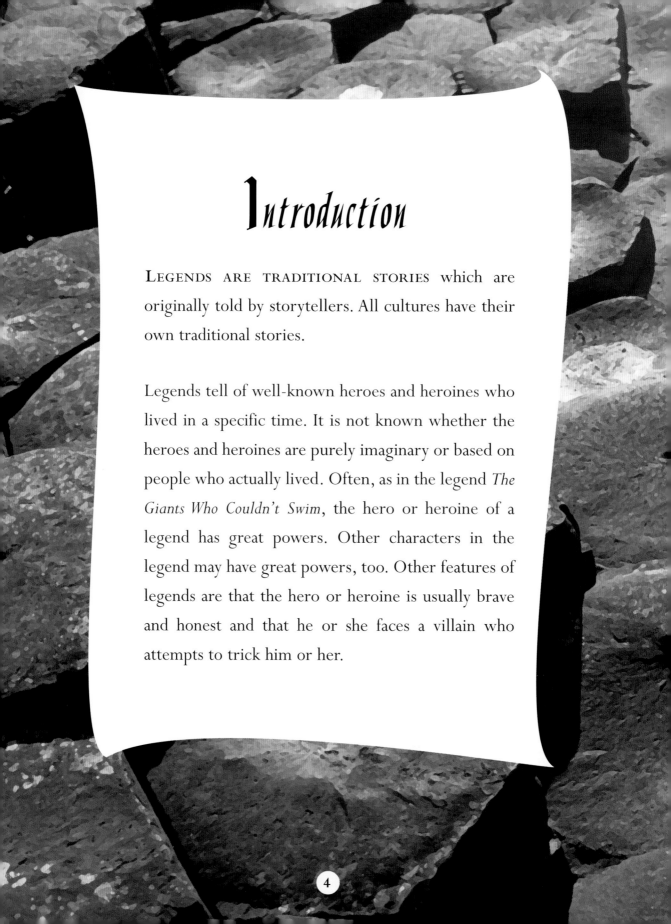

Introduction

LEGENDS ARE TRADITIONAL STORIES which are originally told by storytellers. All cultures have their own traditional stories.

Legends tell of well-known heroes and heroines who lived in a specific time. It is not known whether the heroes and heroines are purely imaginary or based on people who actually lived. Often, as in the legend *The Giants Who Couldn't Swim*, the hero or heroine of a legend has great powers. Other characters in the legend may have great powers, too. Other features of legends are that the hero or heroine is usually brave and honest and that he or she faces a villain who attempts to trick him or her.

Features of a Legend

LEGENDS ARE STORIES IN WHICH:

- the hero or heroine lived in a specific time and sometimes had great powers

- the story line is fast-paced and full of action

- the hero or heroine is usually brave and honest

- there is a villain who tries to trick or defeat the hero or heroine

- the characters may be based on people who lived in the past. Examples are Robin Hood and his band of thieves or King Arthur and the Knights of the Round Table.

The Flight of ICARUS

Introduction

ICARUS WAS THE SON of Daedalus, an architect and sculptor in ancient Greece. There are many stories about Daedalus in Greek **mythology**. He designed and built the **labyrinth** of the Minotaur for King Minos of Crete. The labyrinth is a maze of winding passages, which make it impossible to find the way out. The Minotaur was a fearsome monster that the king imprisoned in the labyrinth.

Archaeologists have discovered the remains of a building that may have been this labyrinth—called the Cretan Labyrinth.

The labyrinth of the Minotaur, built by Daedalus

After building this amazing labyrinth, Daedalus offended King Minos. The king was furious and locked up Daedalus and Icarus. In order to escape from their prison, Daedalus made two sets of wings out of candle wax and feathers so they could escape. Daedalus told his son that as long as they both flew between the sky and the sea, they would be safe.

However, Icarus did not listen to his father, and his actions had terrible consequences …

The Flight of ICARUS

A Greek Legend

ONCE LONG AGO in Greece there lived a famous mechanic named Daedalus. While visiting Crete, King Minos, the ruler of the island, became angry with him, and ordered him shut up in the high tower that faced the lonely sea. In time, with the help of his young son, Icarus, Daedalus managed to escape from the tower, only to find himself a prisoner on the island. Several times he tried by **bribery** to stow away on one of the **vessels** sailing from Crete, but King Minos kept a strict watch over them and no ships were allowed to sail without being carefully searched.

Daedalus was an **ingenious** artist and was not **discouraged** by his failures. "Minos may control the land and sea," he said, "but he does not control the air. I will try that way."

He called his son Icarus to him and told the boy to gather up all the feathers he could find on the rocky shore. As thousands of gulls soared over the island, Icarus soon collected a huge pile of feathers. Daedalus then melted some wax and made a skeleton in the shape of a bird's wing. The smallest feathers he pressed into the soft wax, and the large ones he tied on with thread. Icarus played about on the beach happily while his father worked, chasing the feathers that blew away in the strong wind that swept the island. And sometimes he took bits of wax and worked it into strange shapes with his fingers.

It was fun making the wings. The sun shone on the bright feathers; the breezes ruffled them. When they were finished, Daedalus fastened them to his shoulders and found himself lifted upwards, where he hung **poised** in the air. Filled with excitement, he made another pair for his son. They were smaller than his own, but strong and beautiful.

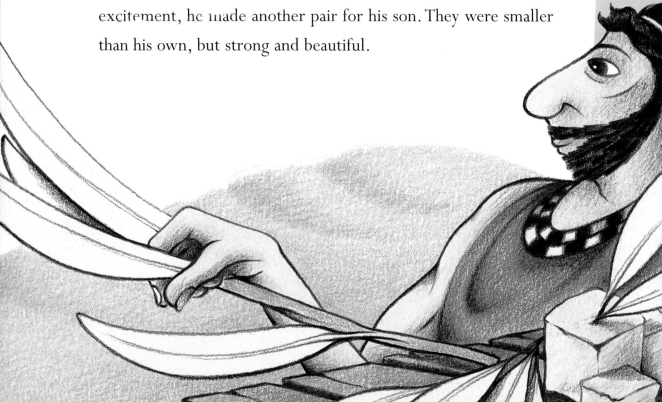

Finally, one clear, wind-swept morning, the wings were finished, and Daedalus fastened them to Icarus's shoulders and taught him how to fly. He **bade** him watch the movements of the birds, how they soared and glided overhead. He pointed out the slow, graceful sweep of their wings as they beat the air steadily, without fluttering. Soon Icarus was sure that he, too, could fly, and, raising his arms up and down, skirted over the white sand and even out over the waves, letting his feet touch the snowy foam as the water thundered and broke over the sharp rocks.

Daedalus watched him proudly but with **misgivings**. He called Icarus to his side, and putting his arm around the boy's shoulders, said, "Icarus, my son, we are about to make our flight. No human being has ever travelled through the air before, and I want you to listen carefully to my instructions. Keep at **moderate** height, for if you fly too low, the fog and **spray** will **clog** your wings, and if you fly too high, the heat will melt the wax that holds them together. Keep near me and you will be safe."

He kissed Icarus and fastened the wings more securely to his son's shoulders. Icarus, standing in the bright sun, the shining wings drooping gracefully from his shoulders, his golden hair wet with spray and his eyes bright and dark with excitement, looked like a lovely bird. Daedalus's eyes filled with tears and, turning away, he soared into the sky and called to Icarus to follow. From time to time, he looked back to see that the boy was safe and to note how he managed his wings in his flight. As they flew across the land to test their **prowess** before setting out across the dark wild sea, **ploughmen** below stopped their work and shepherds gazed in wonder, thinking Daedalus and Icarus were gods.

Father and son flew over Samos and Delos which lay to their left, and Lebinthus, which lay on their right. Icarus, beating his wings with joy, felt the thrill of the cool wind on his face and the clear air above and below him. He flew higher and higher up into the blue sky until he reached the clouds. His father saw him and called out in alarm. He tried to follow him, but he was heavier and his wings would not carry him.

Up and up Icarus soared, through the soft, moist clouds and out again towards the glorious sun. He was bewitched by a sense of freedom and beat his wings frantically, so that they would carry him higher and higher to heaven itself. The blazing sun beat down on the wings and softened the wax. Small feathers fell from the wings and floated softly down, warning Icarus to stay his flight and glide to Earth. But the enchanted boy did not notice them until the sun became so hot that the largest feathers dropped off and he began to sink. Frantically, he fluttered his arms, but no feathers remained to hold the air. He cried out to his father, but his voice was submerged in the blue waters of the sea, which has forever been called by his name.

Daedalus, crazed by anxiety, called back to him, "Icarus! Icarus, my son, where are you?" At last he saw the feathers floating from the sky and soon his son plunged through the clouds into the sea. Daedalus hurried to save him, but it was too late. He gathered the boy in his arms and flew to land, the tips of his wings dragging in the water from the double **burden** they bore. Weeping bitterly, he buried his small son and called the land Icaria in his memory.

Then, with a flutter of his wings, he once more took to the air, but the joy of his flight was gone and his victory over the air was bitter to him. He arrived safely in Sicily, where he built a temple to Apollo and hung up his wings as an offering to the god.

THE GIANTS
Who Couldn't Swim

Introduction

LOOK AT THE MAP of the coasts of Scotland and Northern Ireland. The arrow points to the area where the Giant's **Causeway** is found. This natural wonder gets its name from the following legend, which tells the story of a giant, Finn MacCool. He is said to have built the causeway as a road to Scotland.

The Causeway is actually an unusual formation of rock columns along the north coast of County Antrim in Northern Ireland. There are about 40 000 separate columns that are quite close together. Some of the pillars measure up to seven metres high and are about forty to fifty centimetres round (or in **circumference**). **Geologists** believe that the Causeway resulted from lava flow from a volcano.

After reading the story, decide which explanation *you* like the best.

The Giant's Causeway, Northern Ireland

THE GIANTS
Who Couldn't Swim

An Irish Legend

THIS IS THE STORY OF TWO GIANTS. One lived all alone in a cave in Scotland, on a rocky island called Staffa. He was called Bennadonner. The other lived with his wife in a snug stone house on the wild north coast of Antrim, in Ireland. His name was Finn MacCool.

Both the giants had magical powers. Finn had a Thumb of Knowledge which told him what to do when he got into a muddle. He simply sucked it like a baby, and the right answer came to him. Bennadonner had a Magic Finger which let him see into the future, and which warned him when trouble was **brewing**.

When Finn MacCool was young he'd fallen in love with a beautiful giantess who lived next door to Bennadonner, on his rocky island. The problem was that he couldn't swim so he chopped down a forest and built a huge boat so that he could sail across the Irish Sea.

But it sank the minute he set foot in it, for he weighed as much as a small mountain.

For a while he couldn't think how to cross the water. Then he had an idea. He gathered together some huge pieces of rock, tall columns with six sides, like **honeycombs**, but with smooth flat tops, and put them in the sea, making a great road of stepping stones. This stretched from Antrim in Ireland to Staffa in Scotland, and he proudly called it "The Giant's Causeway".

For many years Finn and his lovely wife Oonagh lived at home in peace. In his cave sat Bennadonner, staring out **wistfully** across the sea. He was lonely in his cave and he wanted a wife too.

One stormy morning he sent a message across to Finn, challenging him to a fight, and saying he would be over to see him as soon as the sea was calm again, and not slopping over the Causeway. (No giant likes getting his feet wet, and Bennadonner couldn't swim either.)

Finn read the challenge to Oonagh, and they both roared with laughter. They shook so much that down in the village all the chimney pots fell off, and the people put up their shutters against a storm. "Let him come!" laughed Finn, making a pen out of a small fir tree and scribbling a message on his wife's best table cloth. "Let's fight! We'll soon see who's the stronger." And the meeting was fixed for the very next fine day.

Sure enough, one sunny morning Bennadonner set off for Antrim across the Giant's Causeway. Finn had gone for a walk before dinner, just a little stroll right across the Six Counties, so when Bennadonner reached his house the Irish giant was many miles from home.

Oonagh shouted to him across the mountains when she saw the Scottish giant prowling round the house, and Finn rushed back towards Antrim. His feet were so large that lakes formed where his shoes sank in the mud. He was rather looking forward to meeting **puny** Bennadonner, and to putting him in his place. But when he reached home he saw with horror that two huge footprints had been freshly made outside the door, *footprints at least as huge as his own!*

Finn shook with nerves, and the whole of Ireland trembled. This meant that Bennadonner was as big as he was! But how could this be? Wasn't Finn MacCool the biggest giant in the whole world? He sucked his magic thumb but for once no bright idea came to him. So he hurried inside to ask his wife's advice.

"Stop sucking your thumb, Finn," she told him severely, and she set his dinner before him. This began with sixteen duck eggs, eight pigs' trotters and three raw onions to help digest the meal. Then she brought in a piece of roast meat so huge it covered the whole table. But Finn was off his food. All he could think of was Bennadonner **skulking** about outside in the darkness.

He was sucking his thumb again, and trying not to cry, when somebody knocked at the door so hard the whole house shook to its **foundations**. "It's Bennadonner!" he **whimpered**, clinging to Oonagh. "What am I going to do?"

His wife pulled out a cradle from under the table. It had once belonged to their son Ossian, but he'd long since gone to live with the fairies, and was learning to be a poet. "Get into it!" she ordered, giving him a poke.

"I'm too big!" he protested.

"Well, you'll just have to double up," she said, stuffing him in, "or treble up." And she whisked a blanket over him as the door creaked open and Bennadonner strode into the room.

He was a horrible sight. He was every bit as big as the handsome red-haired Finn who now lay squashed in the cradle by the fire, sucking his thumb, and trying to look like a baby. He was dressed in the skins of rats and skunks and he had a third eye in the middle of his forehead which rolled about hideously when he spoke.

"Where is Finn MacCool?" Bennadonner roared.

Oonagh was all sweetness. "He's out walking, Mr Bennadonner," she said, "but he'll be back shortly. Sit yourself down, do, and let me offer you some food and drink."

She set a **tankard** before him as big as a washing tub, then went to the fire to turn over the flat round **oaten** cakes which she was cooking on an iron **griddle**. As she worked, the giant glanced at the gently rocking cradle. "That's a fine baby you have there, madam," he said.

"To be sure," she answered, "he's but a few weeks old, and no teeth yet."

Bennadonner, biting on his magic finger, suddenly knew that danger was near, and thought of Finn MacCool. "Where is your man?" he demanded more roughly. "Is he hiding from me?"

"*Hiding?*" Oonagh said scornfully. "My Finn *hide?* Why, he's twice the giant you are."

"Oh, *really?*" said Bennadonner, getting angrily to his feet. "I have three times his strength."

"Have you now?" Oonagh said coolly. "Could you turn my house round, for example?"

The giant went straight out into the darkness, lifted up the great stone house from its foundations, and turned it so that it faced the opposite way, with its back to the sea. While he was outside Oonagh slipped a spare griddle into one of the oaten cakes and fetched a freshly made white cheese from her dairy. She had plans to deal with Bennadonner. But Finn was less confident. He burrowed down into his blankets and sucked his magic thumb very hard.

"Have some oaten cakes, do, Mr Bennadonner," Oonagh **wheedled**. He had turned the house round for sure, but she still believed she could outwit him, and send him packing. The giant took a big bite and growled horribly, spitting out two teeth. "What kind of oaten cake is *this?*" he demanded.

"Oh, the softest and finest to be sure," purred Oonagh. "See, the baby likes it well enough." Into Finn's hand she slipped a piece of oaten cake that had no griddle iron in it. He munched it all up in a flash, and made gurgling baby noises.

Bennadonner's mouth dropped open. What kind of baby could this be? "But you said he had no *teeth*," he spluttered, "and your oaten cakes are as hard as iron."

"I did surely," Oonagh said easily, "and he has not. But his little gums are hard. Here, feel for yourself," and she thrust the giant's right hand into Finn's mouth.

He promptly bit off Bennadonner's magic finger. "Aargh!" roared Bennadonner, hopping about in pain. "It's no baby in that cradle, madam, it's a fiend."

"Indeed, 'tis nothing but a baby. But he's strong, sir, like his father, let me show you. He can squeeze water out of a stone."

Into Finn's hand she slipped the round white cheese, new from the dairy, and as he squeezed it, the **whey** dripped down.

Bennadonner's three eyes bulged in his head, and he immediately tried to do the same. But **cunning** Oonagh had given him a white stone, and all he managed to do was to break his remaining fingers.

This was too much for the Scottish giant. If Finn MacCool's baby was as strong as this, what must the father be like?

He turned and ran out of the house, down to the shore and tore back to Staffa just as fast as he could, across the Giant's Causeway. But as he did so, he ripped up the great slippery stones and flung them into the sea. He didn't want Finn MacCool to come visiting *him*.

And that is why there are only two bits of the Causeway left now—on Staffa, in Scotland, and in Ireland, on the rocky Antrim coast. You can go and look at them for yourself, if you don't believe me.

If you should see them, remember this: you'd still be able to walk right across the Irish Sea, without getting your feet wet, if it weren't for those two giants who couldn't swim.

Glossary

The Flight of Icarus

archaeologists   people who study history by digging up and describing remains

bade   to have commanded or told

bribery   offering money, gifts or favours to someone in return for doing something for you

burden   a heavy or difficult load to carry

clog   to block

discouraged   put off, lost hope or confidence

ingenious   clever at inventing things

labyrinth   a twisted maze of confusing paths from which it is hard to escape

misgivings   feelings of doubt, fear or worry

moderate   not great, between little and large

mythology   all the ancient stories of a particular culture

ploughmen   men who work on the land, farmers

poised   confident, balanced and steady

prowess   an outstanding skill or courage

vessels   ships or large boats

spray   a liquid, such as sea water, blown through the air as fine drops

The Giants Who Couldn't Swim

brewing   developing or forming

causeway   a raised road or path across wet or swampy ground

circumference   the length of the outer line of a circle

cunning   clever, using tricks to get what you want

foundations   anything on which something rests or is based

geologists   people who study the layers of rock that form the Earth

griddle   a flat iron plate used for cooking on top of a stove

honeycombs   structures of wax made by honeybees

oaten   made from oats, grain used to feed horses and to make cereal or other foods

puny   not very strong or large

skulking   staying near a place or in the background, hoping that nobody will notice you

tankard   a large mug, with a handle and hinged lid

wheedled   persuaded or obtained by being charming to someone

whey   the watery part of milk that separates from the curd during cheese-making

whimpered   made a weak cry

wistfully   sadly, with disappointment